The Smallest Efficiency Guide in the World:

A guide for busy people who solve problems for a living

By Geir Agustsson

Table of Contents

INTRODUCTION 5

WHAT IS BEING EFFICIENT? 6

   Being competent in what you do 6

   Being able to establish realistic deadlines for your assignments and keep them 6

   Making sure that you are a part of the "flow", and not a bottleneck for anyone 6

   Knowing when a decision can be taken, and when not 7

   Doing things fast *and* well 7

   Doing things well the first time 7

   Creating value – all the time 8

USEFUL ROUTINES 9

   E-mails: Use them intelligently 9

   Communication tools: Choose them well 10

   Value creation: Know how to maximize it 10

   Know when to do what 11

   A clean desk and an organized archive – or not 12

   Create a good working environment................13

   Keep your energy up..13

   Compartmentalize 14

   Don't rely on your memory 14

THINGS TO REMEMBER..16

- Keep your focus 16
- Maintain your health 16
- Don't be a disturbance 16
- Take care of your personal relations 17
- Track your tasks 17
- Prioritize 18
- Choose your words 18
- Assume nothing 18

PITFALLS **20**
- Saying yes to too many assignments with the same deadline 20
- Doing everything yourself: If you can outsource in a clever way, do it! 20
- Attempting to recycle other peoples poorly done job 20
- Attempting too extensive multitasking 21
- Using too much energy on hating the "system" 21
- Doing things in a rush 22
- All work, no play 22
- Neglecting your health 22
- Getting stuck in the present 23

IN CONCLUSION **24**
APPENDIX **25**
- Copyright 25

Acknowledgments..25
About the author 26

Introduction

This is a short guide on efficiency. It does not contain many sentences, but each sentence is considered important. I suggest you read it all through once, and then learn it gradually by applying it in your work, should this interest the reader.

The author considers this short guide equally applicable for employees, managers and entrepreneurs, although the wording is mostly directed towards employees. It can be used directly as a tool at work and as a guide for managers to improve employee efficiency as well as their own.

You read these pages in less than 20 minutes. You will earn those minutes back many times, for you and others.

What is being efficient?

Being competent in what you do

Understandably, you need to have relevant training to be able to do the job well and be efficient. Training can come from school, previous or current work or something else. If you feel you can't do the job and do it like one of the best of them (in a foreseeable future), consider getting another job!

Being able to establish realistic deadlines for your assignments and keep them

This is important but sometimes difficult and that is fine. If you are a part of a team, you need to know when you can finish your tasks, or report back with a new delivery date as soon as you have an estimate. It's all about managing expectations of those depending on your work.

Making sure that you are a part of the "flow", and not a bottleneck for anyone

This is very important. Don't put yourself in a position where you are always explaining why you haven't delivered. Make sure your assignments gain progress, either directly with your work or with your help on others' assignments.

Saying "I don't know, ask someone else" right away is much better than giving no answer at all.

Knowing when a decision can be taken, and when not

You should preferably be the one who knows best how to proceed with your own assignments and what is sufficient in order to proceed. Sometimes this requires input or decisions from others (e.g. the client, your manager or your employees, depending on your situation), and you should know when this is the case. Make sure you take decisions that are part of your job and do it as fast as possible, after gathering required facts and opinions.

Doing things fast *and* well

Of course! But speed is not the first priority.

Doing things well the first time

Sometimes, you waste more time on re-doing things that were done badly than it would have taken you to do things well the first time. Time spent on preparation is often better than time spent on repairing things gone wrong and usually more cost and time effective. The more efficient you are, the less re-work you face. Put differently: If you're efficient, you hardly ever do any re-work.

Creating value – all the time

The efficient worker (employee, manager or entrepreneur) does not have a lot of idle time. He is always creating value when he's at work. There is usually always work to be done. Apparent idle time can be used on future improvements, training, planning future work, simplifying work processes or just basic cleaning and sorting for later and busier times.

Useful routines

Being efficient at work requires a certain amount of discipline. Here are a few routines that could be useful.

E-mails: Use them intelligently

Try to maintain e-mail threads when possible. When sending an e-mail on something that has been discussed via e-mail previously, it can be beneficial to do it with a reply on the last (relevant) e-mail in an e-mail correspondence. The alternative is sometimes to start a fresh thread which forces the recipient to dig up the previous correspondence history.

Keep an eye on your e-mails to an extent that doesn't distract you too much, but don't reply them all as soon as they come in. Some e-mails can wait, but many are good to get out of the way. The same actually applies for telephone calls, but it's considered rude not to answer your telephone so you better do that. Quick replies to urgent e-mails can also reduce the telephone call frequency.

In general it's a good idea to avoid sending e-mails which require a lot of work for the recipient to understand, e.g. by referring obscurely to old discussions or huge documents without further guidelines or information. Try to find a balance between being detailed and not writing too much text. Reference relevant background material when this is applicable. Help your recipient to understand what is expected of him or her with your e-mail.

Communication tools: Choose them well

Try to refrain from being an endless "caller" - making a phone call every time you strike a thought you want to share or pass on. Telephone calls are very intrusive (as it is considered rude not to take them). Make a call from you important, so that people know that if you call, it truly is important.

Meetings (formal or informal) can be very useful but they can also be a pure waste of time. Make an agenda and stick to it. Minimize the number of participants on the meeting and the scope of the meeting itself. Open agendas like "brainstorming" often end up being brain-wasting.

Try to keep your private and professional correspondence separated, e.g. by directing private e-mails to a separate and private e-mail address or filter them from your work in-box into a separate folder. For some it could be useful to maintain separate telephones for work and home.

Value creation: Know how to maximize it

Know when to stop. Some assignments can always be worked on, indefinitely, but at some point you need to stop and deliver. It's a balance between value creation and perfection. Both have to be there, but at some point the perfection starts eating away on the value creation.

Try to invest time to save time: Sometimes you need to sharpen the ax before chopping the tree. So evaluate when you want to invest and use time on something that will, in the long run, save both you and others time and effort. Is the document template bad and always needs fixing? Update the template! Are you doing repetitive work, e.g. copy-paste work from one document to another? Figure out a way to automate that, e.g. by writing a small program or have one made for you which performs the given tasks, or buy or lease a smarter tool.

Know when to do what

During some days, you just know that you cannot cope with your most challenging tasks. For some, Mondays are difficult. If you go out for a few beers you know that the brain is slower the day after. Some days have many and/or long meetings. Try to arrange your to-do list in such a way that you fit the "easy" tasks on the lesser brain effective days.

Try to have your priorities in order. You can't do everything at once. Try to have a continuous and open dialogue with your manager or client and agree with him on what is important, and why. Otherwise, you might end up using a lot of time on explaining why you haven't delivered yet.

Some parts of the day are more useful than others. For many, the afternoons can't be used for any work of real value. The body is tired, the calls from home begin, the plans for the evening begin to unfold, or the people you work with begin to get restless and want to talk more. If you want a long day, try to show up early or be back at work after dinner. For others, e.g. those who have a lot of meetings during the day, the afternoons are a prime time and should be kept as peaceful as possible.

A clean desk and an organized archive – or not

This is always a huge emphasis in all courses on efficiency and work processes. In reality, stuff can be categorized into two groups: Stuff only you use, and stuff you share with others. It does not matter where you put your own stuff, as long as you know where it is. Stuff you share with others should be in places known by all its users, of course. This simple fact is the core of all (longer) programs on work processes, and sufficient as well.

Try to throw away papers and things you don't need if they take up too much space. The trash bin is often the most useful of all organizing devices, as is the delete-button on your keyboard.

Create a good working environment

Some people like to work in a busy room, others don't. If you can influence this, do it. If you are forced to work in a busy room and you don't like it, try headphones with noise cancellation and some loud music in your tempo. Just make sure you can see/feel/hear your telephone ring and preferably indicate to the people around you that you can't hear them call your name, so a poke in the shoulder is required to obtain your attention.

The same applies for your e-mail in-box and computer desktop: Find a system for you. Many like a clean in-box and a dirty desktop, or the other way around, while others like everything clean. There is no universal formula for all, but in general you should try to know what is relevant and active in your work, and what is just plain historic remains and mess.

Keep your energy up

For some, this means an eight hour sleep and an hour of day in the gym. For other, it just means a lot of coffee and water. Find out what works for you. And if you can foresee a day with low energy, try to put the less-demanding assignments on it. Every minute at work counts, but not all minutes are equally demanding of you.

Compartmentalize

Some days at home are tough. This should not affect your work day though. Try to maintain a working spirit at work no matter what.

This also applies the other way around. Some days at the work place are tough. You got disturbed all the time and didn't get any planned work done. You got stuck on a difficult problem. You come home, not happy about your working day. Try to keep this from affecting your life at home.

In general it is a good mental practice to try to keep things in mental "boxes" with little emotional overlap. It can be a difficult exercise, but can become a rewarding one.

Don't rely on your memory

A good memory is an extremely useful tool to have.

Try, however, to work on the assumption that you won't remember anything you did in a few days, weeks or years (depending on the context). This means constant considerations to traceability of your work, making clear notes and documenting in an organized way when applicable. Adhering to this means you can always resume work on something you did earlier without spending time on figuring out what is what or re-inventing the wheel.

This will have the added benefit of helping others to take over from you or use your work for something else.

Things to remember

Keep your focus

Try to keep your focus intact. If you lose it, try regaining it by taking a short walk or have a glass of water, a cup of coffee or a piece of fruit.

Maintain your health

It is difficult to be efficient if you are not well physically and mentally. Try to enjoy your work, colleagues and clients and promote a good working morale. You can also help the people around you be efficient by helping them feel good and create a good moral within the company.

Try to do what you think is needed to maintain your physical health, e.g. stand up regularly or stretch at work. You can also exercise in various ways both outside and inside of work, e.g. by taking the stairs instead of the elevator, bicycle to and from work or go to a gym.

For short and long term efficiency it is better to look after both your body and soul.

Don't be a disturbance

Don't disturb others unless you need to, but don't waste time on something which takes you a long time if others can help you do it quickly. It's a thin line! Don't give up too quickly, but don't waste valuable time.

It is normal and very acceptable to seek assistance and advice, but pay attention when you do and take your time to listen to your advisor and write down or keep track of what you need to know.

Take care of your personal relations

Try to be friendly. You don't get too far if you don't take care of your personal relations. They can also be a reward in themselves, be a means to an end, and an end in themselves.

Track your tasks

You should always keep track of your tasks. Preferably, you only need to be given a task once, and after that you keep track of it and take responsibility for it. You don't "forget" it or neglect it. You know all your actions all the time. If something is not important anymore, e.g. because time has elapsed and everything changed, you strike the task from your list on purpose. You might have a manager, project manager or a very detailed-oriented client, but none of those should be responsible for your tasks, their status, progress or way forward on them.

If you for some reason are not the one to finish what you started, you should be able to pass your assignment or project on in an organized way (including deadlines, priorities, stakeholders and present status).

Prioritize

Not everything is equally important in the short and long run. Try to have an idea of what is important and when. Urgent short-term assignments will normally take up most of your time, but you should always try to plan yourself out of "firefighting" assignments with a more prophetic long-term plan so that nothing of importance (short-term and long-term) falls between any cracks.

You might need input from your manager, client or employees to prioritize and help manage expectations and should not refrain from obtaining this. The client, for example, can and often will shift his priorities and you should be on top of that.

Choose your words

Not everyone has to know your' every single thought on every single subject. Try to say less and get attention when you talk rather than talk all the time and gradually become filtered out of dialogues (in effect ignored).

Assume nothing

Assuming something can be a leap of faith. You may assume others have your phone number, that meeting attendees have read relevant background material or are available at times of need without any planning.

There are many ways to guard yourself against unfounded assumptions. You can include your telephone number as a signature on all your e-mails. You can emphasize the importance of coming prepared to your meetings. You can try to estimate the time and place for when you need certain people at your disposal and make sure they are available.

Pitfalls

Here are some pitfalls that have trapped many busy problem-solving people.

Saying yes to too many assignments with the same deadline

In the end, you won't be able to complete anything or do anything well. Everything stagnates at a 75% completion ratio. Nobody wins.

Doing everything yourself: If you can outsource in a clever way, do it!

Good employees have a tendency to get a lot of assignments. Sometimes it makes sense to chop your assignments into small, clearly and well defined pieces and try to get help with them. This will backfire if you forget the "clearly and well defined" part of the outsourcing because you end up getting so many questions that the time you wanted to save is used up. So make sure you outsource in an organized way.

Attempting to recycle other peoples poorly done job

It is always tempting to try to save time by building your work on other peoples work, e.g. base your report on someone others old report.

If you choose a poor template or foundation for

your work, you will end up using a lot of your time fixing and changing and you save nothing. Recycling does not always pay off (not even in the long run), despite the propaganda. It becomes "junk in, junk out".

Attempting too extensive multitasking

They say that only women can multitask. That is not true. Nobody can in reality multitask. However, working on many separate tasks during a short time interval is possible. Try to divide your day, week or month into "slots" for each of them. Try to have each slot as large as possible, whether it is measured in hours, days or weeks. The aim should be that the size of each slot is enough to start and finish a task or project, or at least reach a milestone in it, but sometimes this is very unrealistic. It takes time to switch between tasks, at least those that require brain-power. That time is a waste of time, so try to minimize it.

Using too much energy on hating the "system"

The system is what it is, for whatever reason. You should try to change things that don't work and you can expect to change, and invent things that do work, but you shouldn't decide on your own that "the system" is no good and use a lot of energy on that thought.

Nobody likes to take off their shoes and belt in the

airport, but we do it anyway, or else we don't get through. We pay taxes to stay out of jail. We can try to influence "the system" but while it is what it is, it is what it is.

Doing things in a rush

"That which is done well enough is done fast enough", said a wise man once. This is a good motto. If you have to re-do something, you have wasted time. Try to do everything correct and well the first time. Be thorough, ensure that your work is traceable and think about what you write or present. Time invested on this is time well spent. Time invested on something poorly done is usually wasted time.

All work, no play

You, as a human being, need to take a break on a regular basis. Make plans to look forward to. Working hard is easier if you have a venue to play hard as well. It doesn't have to be anything special, just a break in the routine, a relaxing moment or a party with a few friends. "Work hard, play hard" is a really useful and practical motto, even if the "hard" part in "play hard" is not so hard.

Neglecting your health

A loss of health – mental or physical – is a loss of energy, focus and endurance. It is really that simple.

Getting stuck in the present

The only reason you get paid as an employee, contractor or entrepreneur in the private sector is because you create more value for your employer or customer than you cost him. The only way you can expect an ever-increasing salary or reward in the future is if you increase your value-creating abilities. Experience or a certain reputation is sometimes not enough. People often assume that they automatically become more valuable with time. This is not correct.

Try to gradually add to your value-creating skills, either in your job or spare time. This could mean learning a new programming language, or taking a course in management, investing in new technology or equipment, or just dig deeper into your own work, e.g. by expanding the scope of your expertise or increasing the depth of your knowledge and work.

In conclusion

To become more effective is a lifelong task and a mental process that should never stop. There will always be room for improvements. Having a mindset that strives towards smarter solutions and more efficiency will bring you ever-increasing salary, more job satisfaction and more professional popularity. It will bring you a sense of growth and development that will make all the hard work seem worth it. It will encourage you to continue on this path. It will make you think of your job or profession as an enjoyable part of your day rather than a nuisance or a burden or a necessary evil.

APPENDIX

Copyright

© Copyright 2014 by Geir Agustsson. All rights reserved.

Acknowledgments

First, I would like to thank my wife for her endless support and inspiration. And my family deserves thanks for keeping me very busy at home, or even away from home, thereby forcing me to adjust to a limited amount of time for an ever-increasing work load.

Secondly, I would like to thank those who helped me with this little book by giving me useful comments and suggestions. You know who you are! (I, of course, take full responsibility for any errors or potentially bad advice in this book.)

Thirdly, I would like to thank my employer for the last 10 years for never giving me a dull moment.

And last but not least, I would like to thank my friends and colleagues throughout my life. I have learned so much from you, and will continue to do so.

About the author

This author is an engineer with a decade of engineering work experience on his back. He is a married man with two children, and has a demanding job.

Combining family and work has perhaps been the most challenging work of his life, and has forced him to make the most he can with the time he has.

www.ingramcontent.com/pod-product-compliance
Lightning Source LLC
Chambersburg PA
CBHW070734180526
45167CB00004B/1747